Code It
Yourself

MAKING

MUSIC FROM SCRATCH

An Augmented Reading Experience

Download the Capstone app!

- Ask an adult to download the Capstone 4D app.

- Scan the cover and stars inside the book for additional content.

When you scan a spread, you'll find
fun extra stuff to go with this book!
You can also find these things
on the web at www.capstone4D.com
using the password: coding.music

Dabble Lab is published by Capstone Press
1710 Roe Crest Drive
North Mankato, Minnesota 56003
www.mycapstone.com

Library of Congress Cataloging-in-Publication Data
Names: Ziter, Rachel author.
Title: Making music from Scratch / by Rachel Ziter.
Description: North Mankato, Minnesota : Capstone Press, 2018. | Series: Dabble lab. Code it yourself 4D | Series: 4D an augmented reading experience
Identifiers: LCCN 2018010608 (print) | LCCN 2018013344 (ebook) | ISBN 9781515766636 (eBook PDF) | ISBN 9781515766605 (hardcover) | ISBN 9781543536126 (pbk.)
Subjects: LCSH: Scratch (Computer program language)—Juvenile literature. | Computer music–Instruction and study—Juvenile. | Computer programming—Juvenile literature.
Classification: LCC ML74.4.S37 (ebook) | LCC ML74.4.S37 Z57 2018 (print) | DDC 781.3/45133–dc23
LC record available at https://lccn.loc.gov/2018010608

Designer: Heidi Thompson

Photo Credits
Shutterstock: AlexZaitsev, Cover, Kotkoa, Cover, Phil's Mommy, 6
"Scratch is a trademark of Massachusetts Institute of Technology, which does not sponsor, endorse, or authorize this content. See scratch.mit.edu for more information."

Table of Contents

INTRODUCTION

MUSIC PROJECTS

CODING EXTRAS

What Is Coding?

Playing with an app on your smartphone. Clicking through a website. Without even realizing it, you're using coding. Coding is the language used to communicate with a computer. By creating a set of code, you're writing directions in a language that the computer can follow. Although computers may seem super smart, that's not the case! The only reason computers know how to do *anything* is because they have been coded to do it. A computer's code—the very specific directions given by a person—allows it to be the super-smart device we all know and love. The reality is, anyone can learn to code. In this book we'll be creating projects using one coding language in particular: Scratch.

What Is Scratch?

Scratch is an online coding platform that uses colorful coding blocks to create everything from games to presentations to animation. The colored blocks are sorted into categories like **Motion**, **Looks**, and **Sound**. By connecting the colorful blocks, you can start coding whatever comes to mind. For example, if you want to code a character to move around and make noise, you would start with an **Events** block, then add a **Motion** block, and finish with a **Sound** block. (You can also use a Control block to make the events repeat as many times as you'd like.)

Scratch runs on Adobe Flash Player, so make sure your software is up-to-date.
To download and install Flash, go to: https://get.adobe.com/flashplayer/

TIP:

The projects in this book build in complexity. If you've never coded before, start with the first project and work your way through. If something doesn't make sense in a later project, try going back to earlier projects to find the answer.

Creating a Scratch Account

To create the projects in this book, you will need a Scratch account. To get started, go to: www.scratch.mit.edu. In the upper right corner, click the *Join Scratch* button.

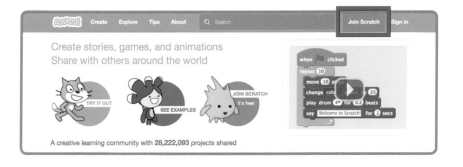

A window will pop up and ask you to create a Scratch username and password. Pick a password you can remember.

It's easy (and free!) to sign up for a Scratch account.

Choose a Scratch Username		Don't use your real name
Choose a Password		
Confirm Password		

The next window will ask for your birth month/year. This is just to make sure you are old enough to use Scratch. If you are younger than 12, you'll need a parent's email to get permission.

Your responses to these questions will be kept private.
Why do we ask for this info

Birth Month and Year	- Month -	- Year -
Gender	○Male ○Female ○	
Country	- Country -	

The next window will ask for an email address. Scratch will send one email—to confirm your email address—when you sign up. After that, you'll only get emails if you need to reset your password.

Enter your email address and we will send you an email to confirm your account.

Email address

Confirm email address

☐ Receive updates from the Scratch Team

How to Use Scratch

Once you've created your Scratch account, you will see your username in the top right corner of the Scratch homepage. If you don't see your username, you need to sign in. Click *sign in* and enter the username and password that you've created.

SCRATCH   Create   Explore   Tips   About   🔍 Search   ✉   📁   🐱   ⌄

Press *create* to start working on a new project.

If you've visited Scratch previously, click on this folder to access projects you've already started working on or finished.

You can also search other games and projects on Scratch. This can be a fun way to get inspiration for new projects and see all the possibilities of what can be created in Scratch! Try searching for a project similar to one you'd like to make, then open the existing project to see what code was used.

When you click *create*, your screen will look like this:

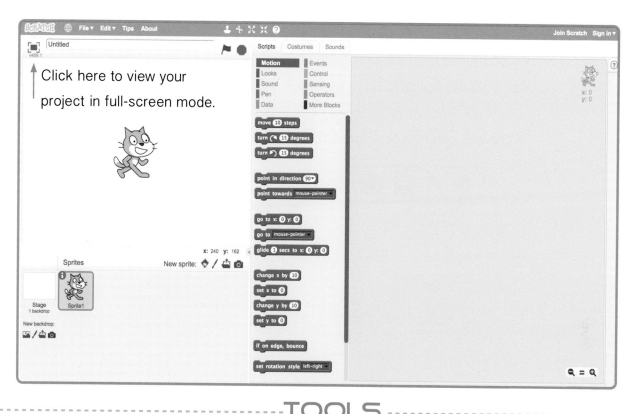

TOOLS

These tools are found at the top of the screen. They are helpful for creating new projects. Click on the tool you want to use—it will turn blue and the mouse will turn into the tool. Then click on the item you'd like to duplicate, cut, grow, or shrink.

 stamp—The stamp is used to duplicate anything in your project. To use this tool, click on the icon so the cursor turns into the stamp, then click whatever you'd like to copy. You can click on a premade character or even a set of code.

 scissors—The scissors are used to delete items in your project.

 outward arrows—The arrows facing outward are used to grow characters. Continue clicking on the character until it is the desired size.

 inward arrows—The arrows facing inward are used to shrink characters. Continue clicking on the character until it is the desired size.

WHAT IS A SPRITE?

A sprite is any moveable character or object used in a project. Sprites can be selected through the Scratch Library, created using drawing tools, or uploaded from the computer. Scratch Cat is an example of a sprite!

All sprites can be accessed in this box:

Sprite Library

NAME YOUR PROJECT HERE

This screen shows you what your project will look like when it's finished.
In this area you can arrange your sprites on top of your background however you'd like for your project.

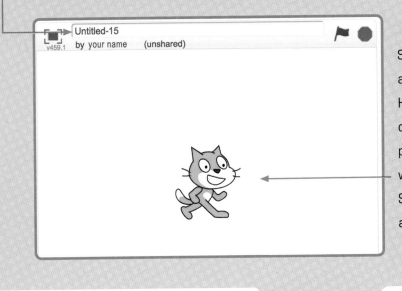

Untitled-15
by your name   (unshared)
v459.1

Scratch Cat will automatically appear on every project you start. He is the face of Scratch. If you don't want to use him in your project, it's OK! You can select whichever sprite you would like. But Scratch Cat will always appear with a new project to get you started.

alien head—Click on the alien head to open the Sprite Library and select a sprite. All sprites are sorted alphabetically. You can choose anything from a dinosaur sprite to cheesy puffs to an airplane.

 paintbrush—Click on the paintbrush to open the paint tools and create your own sprite.

 folder—Click on the folder to upload an image from your computer to use as a sprite.

 camera—Click on the camera to use a picture from your computer as a sprite. A box will pop up asking to access the camera. Press *allow* to let Scratch access your computer's camera.

NAME YOUR SPRITE HERE

Click the blue ℹ to open the sprite's information.

If a sprite is flipping upside down, change its rotation style here.

When you have selected a sprite, you will see three tabs in the top right corner: Scripts, Costumes, and Sounds.

Code blocks are color coded. To figure out which category a certain block is in, look at the color of the block and match it with the category.

SCRIPTS TAB:

The Scripts tab is where you will create the code for all your projects. When you click on the Scripts tab, you will have access to the different code blocks needed to create projects.

Motion: These blocks are used to create movement. Using these blocks, you can tell your sprite to move around the screen, go to a particular place, turn, and more.

Looks: Here you will find the code needed to make your sprite or project change colors, grow, shrink, swap backgrounds, switch costumes, and much more! You can even code your sprite to say or think certain things. (When you code it with a *say* block, a speech bubble will appear above the sprite. The *say* and *think* blocks are here rather than in **Sound** because your sprite won't actually make any noise with these two blocks.)

Sound: Turn up the volume! The blocks in this category add sound to your sprites and/or background.

Pen: These blocks allow your sprites to draw lines wherever they move. (For example, if your sprite moves, then turns 90 degrees four times, you can create a square.) The size, color, and shade of the pen can also be programmed here.

Data: Here you can create variables to use within a project. A variable is a value that can be changed throughout the course of a project. (For example, you can use a variable for the number of lives a sprite has in a game.)

Events: These are your start commands. All code has a start command. This tells the program when it needs to start. These blocks will be the first piece used in any code you write. The most commonly used start command in this book will be the green flag.

Control: These blocks control how long certain things happen and if one thing causes another to start. There are repeat loops, wait commands, cloning blocks, and *if then* statements called conditional statements. (For example, *if* a sprite touches a certain color, *then* it needs to react in a certain way.) The *if then* conditional block will be one of the most used in this book.

Sensing: These blocks are used to detect things—like touching a certain sprite or color—in your code. They are often paired with the *if then* conditional block from Control. (For example, "If touching color blue, then the sprite jumps three times.")

Operators: These code blocks are used to combine codes or set a random range for something within a set of code. They will always be combined with other code blocks when used.

More Blocks: You won't see any blocks in this category at first—that's because you must create any blocks that go here. It can be helpful to create a block when you need to use a big piece of code repeatedly in a set of commands.

- -

In Scratch, code blocks snap together like puzzle pieces. Simply drag the blocks together to make them attach. The code you create will run in whatever order you place the blocks. To take the blocks apart, pull from the bottom and down. If you remove a single piece, all the blocks attached below will stay connected to that piece. (You must pull each one off from the bottom.) To throw away a block you no longer want or need, drag it back to the category you originally selected it from and let go.

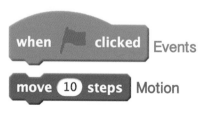

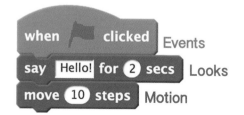

The code block on the right starts with the green flag being clicked. (This is the start command.) Next the sprite will say "Hello!" for two seconds. Once the two seconds have passed, the sprite will move 10 steps.

COSTUMES:

Here you can edit a sprite's appearance. You can also create your own sprite, or add a new costume to an existing sprite. Different costumes can be used to make it look like a sprite is moving. (Some sprites—like Scratch Cat—automatically come with more than one costume.) Multiple costumes are key to making your sprite look animated. Keep in mind that while you may have multiple costumes, there is still only one sprite!

You can name your costumes here.

When you open the Costumes tab, you will see tools you can use to customize your sprite.

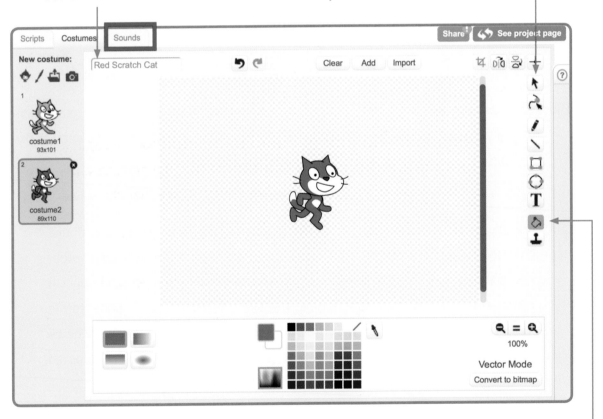

For this costume we used the paint bucket to make Scratch Cat red instead of his usual orange.

BACKDROPS:

Just like with sprites, there are lots of ways to access backdrops in Scratch and make them your own. You can select, create, upload, or snap a picture. The buttons used to create a new backdrop can be found on the bottom left corner of your screen, under the sprites section. There are four buttons you will use:

 mountain landscape—This icon opens the Backdrop Library so you can select a backdrop.

 paintbrush—This icon opens the paint tools, allowing you to create and name your own background.

 folder—This icon lets you upload an image from your computer to use as a background.

 camera—This icon lets you take a picture from your computer and use it as a background. (Note: When you click the camera, a pop-up box will ask to access the camera. Press *allow* to use the camera to create a backdrop.)

Backdrops are sorted by category and alphabetically in the Backdrop Library.

BACKDROP LIBRARY:

How to Use the Sound Tools

Adding sound to your projects is a great way to customize your creations. Scratch has tons of built-in options, but there are also fun ways to create and edit your own sounds. You can even upload them!

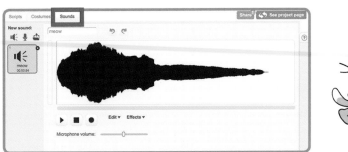

Tip:

Sprites that are imported or created using the graphic design tools do not have any sounds attached. You'll need to add sounds to these sprites.

Once you've started a project, you can add sound. Above is Scratch Cat's Sounds tab. Each sprite comes with one sound preloaded. For Scratch Cat it's *meow.* (Other sprites usually come with simple sounds like *pop.*) When you select a sound, you will see the length of the sound in the area to the right.

The easiest way to add a sound to a project is to select it from the Sound Library. To access the Sound Library, click on the speaker icon.

New sound:

To preview a sound, click on it, then click the play button. To select the sound for your project, click *OK* on the bottom right.

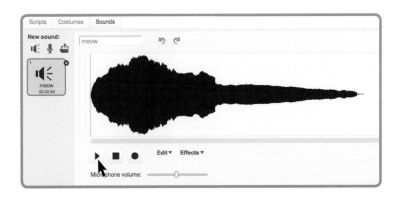

SOUND LIBRARY:

You can use the categories on the left to search within the Sound Library. Sounds are sorted alphabetically to make them easier to find.

There are a few options for sound choices other than selecting one from the Sound Library. If you click the microphone icon, you can record your own sound. A new sound (labeled: *recording 1*) will appear in your list of sounds.

New sound:

microphone

To start recording, click on the circle button.

The first time you do this, you'll see this message:

Clicking *allow* will cause a sound box to appear. When you are recording, the circle will turn red and you'll see a message that says *Recording*. To stop recording, click the square button. The sound you recorded will fill the space.

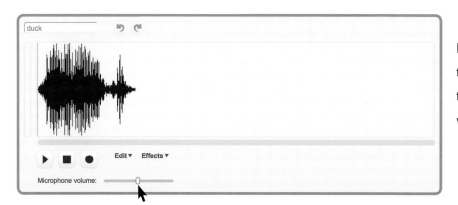

If the sound you were trying to record wasn't picked up, try adjusting the microphone volume on the slider bar.

You can also upload a sound. Make sure it's an mp3 or wav file. You can find a lot of sounds online, but not all are free to download—www.soundbible.com is a good site.

Similar Sound Effects	Listen	License
Wetlands	▶	Attribution 3.0
Radar Detector Beeps	▶	Personal Use Only
Spear Throw	▶	Attribution 3.0
Vintage Phone Ringing	▶	Sampling Plus 1.0
Large Servo Motor	▶	Attribution 3.0
Sound Effect	Listen	License

Use the search bar to help you find the sound you're looking for. Once you've started a search, a list of sounds will appear. You can preview the sounds using the play button.

When you find a sound you like, click on the name to download it. Then click the music note icon labeled MP3.

TIP:

If you get an error message, try uploading one more time, or changing the download type. (Example: If you tried downloading and uploading a WAV file, try downloading and uploading the MP3 file instead.)

Once you've downloaded a sound, click on the upload icon in the new sound panel. A window will open giving you access to the files on your computer. Open the downloads section and find your MP3 file. Select the file, then click *open* at the bottom of the screen.

New sound:

upload

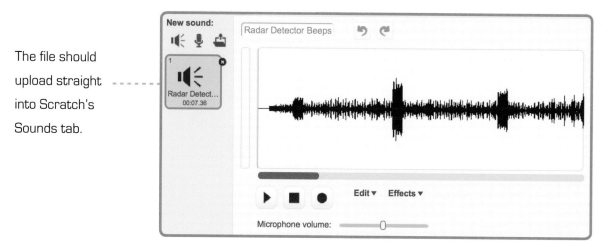

The file should upload straight into Scratch's Sounds tab.

Here you can see the sound uploaded into Scratch. The download's name will appear automatically. To change it, just click inside the box and rename it. (Make sure to credit the sound's creator in your project description!)

EDIT AND EFFECTS

Any sound in Scratch can be changed using the Edit and/or Effects tools. (For this example, we've selected the birthday sound.) To start, select the portion of the sound you want to edit by highlighting it with your mouse.

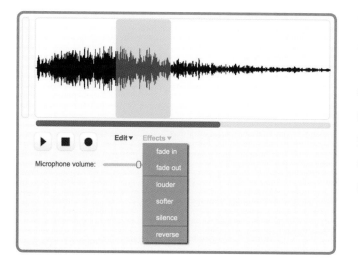

Click on the arrows next to *Edit* and *Effects* to see your options. You can make that portion louder, softer, or silent. If you want to shorten a sound, select **everything except** the part you want to keep. Then use the *cut* option in the *Edit* menu so only the section you want is remaining.

TIP:

If you make a mistake, use *undo* or *redo* in the Edit menu, or use the undo or redo arrows next to the sound name.

Rainbow Piano ★

THE PROJECT:

Create a piano that changes colors when each key plays a note. Whether you are a pianist or just like pressing random keys, this project is a rainbow of sound!

LET'S GET STARTED!

STEP 1: Start a new project and delete Scratch Cat. (Don't forget to name your project!) Use the paintbrush in the new backdrop toolbar to create a new backdrop. It should look something like this:

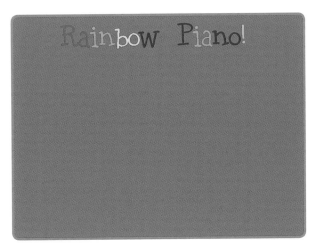

 Use the paint bucket to fill in the background with a solid color of your choice. (A dark color is good so that the rainbow piano keys don't blend in when they are played.)

 Use the text tool to type in *Rainbow Piano!* (You can choose whatever font you'd like at the bottom of the screen.) Make the font larger by stretching the text box with the sizing dots.

 Use the paint bucket to change the color of your rainbow letters.

STEP 2: Click on the paintbrush icon in the sprite toolbar to draw a new sprite. (Make sure you click *convert to vector* at the bottom right before you start drawing!)

 Use the square tool to draw a rectangle outlined in black.

 Use the paint bucket to fill in the rectangle with white.

 In the top left corner, name this first costume *key*.

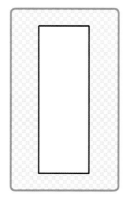

STEP 3: Duplicate the *key* costume using the stamp tool at the top of the screen. You should now have two costumes on the same sprite.

 Use the paint bucket to fill in the second key with a color of your choice.

 In the top left corner, change the name of the new costume to *colored key*. (It's important to always name your costumes. This will make it easier to code changes between them.)

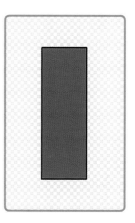

BITMAP MODE VS. VECTOR MODE

There are two different drawing modes in Scratch: **bitmap** and **vector**. Bitmap mode makes it easy to fill in backgrounds and shapes and is good for simple uses. However, in bitmap mode, you won't be able to resize or reshape anything you make. The drawing tools in vector mode are similar to tools in bitmap mode. However, in vector mode you can create another shape and still go back to a previous one and move it. In this mode you can also reshape objects that you have made.

STEP 4: Add the below code to your sprite's Scripts tab:

Use the arrow to select the costume name from the drop-down menu. (If you didn't name your costumes in the earlier steps, the names won't match. Double check those!)

```
when this sprite clicked   Events
switch costume to  colored key ▾   Looks
play note 60▾ for 0.5 beats  Sound
wait 0.2 secs  Control
switch costume to  key ▾   Looks
```

This section of code is activated when the sprite is clicked.

Then the costume switches to the colored key, a note plays, there's a 0.2 second wait, and the costume switches back to the first *key* costume.

If you want the colored key to stay on the screen longer, increase the wait time. Click on the arrow to open the dropdown menu and select the note for your *key* sprite. Start with *Middle C (60)* for this sprite.

STEP 5: Use the stamp tool at the top of the screen to duplicate your sprite (not the costume!) 12 times. You should have 13 sprites at the end of this step.

stamp

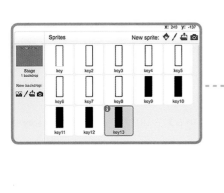

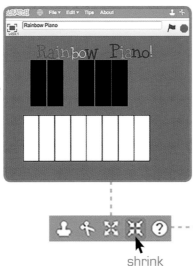

Arrange eight keys together in a line and place five keys on top.

 Go into the Costumes tabs for the five sprites on top and use the paint bucket to make them all black.

Shrink and move the five black keys to finish your piano arrangement!

Using the *shrink* tool, click the sprites until they are the right size.

shrink

STEP 6: In the Costumes tabs of all the white key sprites, use the paint bucket to change the color of the *colored key* costume. Here are the Costume sections for our white keys:

 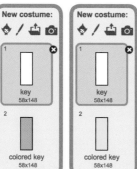  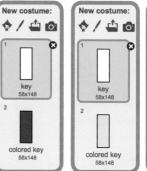  

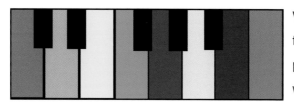

We used a rainbow of colors for the colored keys in this project, but you can pick whatever colors you'd like!

STEP 7: To change the color of the black keys, open the Costumes section of each sprite. Select the *colored key* costume and use the paint bucket and a mixture of two colors to create a cool effect.

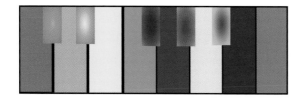

 Click the paint bucket. Select the two colors you want to mix together.

Select how you'd like to mix them. Use the paint bucket to fill in the key.

STEP 8: Because you duplicated your original sprite, each of the key sprites already has this duplicated code. Now you need to change the note each sprite plays.

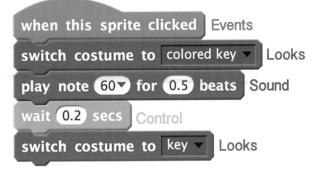

Double click on the key you need to change. Then open the Scripts tab and find the *play note* block. Open the dropdown menu in the **Sound** block and choose the note that matches the key on your piano. Change this code block for all your piano keys so they play the correct note.

Note: You'll only use the last 13 keys on the keyboard in the *play note* code block.

STEP 9: Tweak the code on the black keys so they stay on top of the white keys. The only block you're adding is the *go to front* block from **Looks**. You also need to change the note for each black key in the *play note* block. Do that the same way you did for the white keys in step 8.

This code places the black keys in front of the white keys. When a black key is pressed, it changes its costume to *colored key*, plays the correct note, waits a moment, and then changes back to the regular key costume.

Click on the blue rectangle in the upper left corner to view your project full screen. Play your piano and watch the keys change color! See the finished project here: https://scratch.mit.edu/projects/173770364/

TIP:

If the piano keys aren't changing color properly, go into Scripts and re-select the costume they need to switch to.

⭐ Beach Band

THE PROJECT:

Click on the different instruments to hear the beach band play! To hear all the instruments at once, click the *play all* button.

LET'S GET STARTED!

STEP 1: Start and name your new project. Delete Scratch Cat, then click on the mountain landscape icon in the *New backdrop* toolbar to open the Backdrop Library. Select a beach background for your band.

scissors

Backdrop Library

STEP 2: Open the Sprite Library and choose the instrument sprites for your band. (Repeat until you have as many as you want.) Then select a person sprite so you have someone to dance to the music!

Theme
Castle
City
Dance
Dress-Up
Flying
Holiday
Music
Space
Sports
Underwater
Walking

Sprites in the Sprite Library are sorted by category and alphabetically. Narrow your options to sprites in the music category to make it easier to find what you need.

Sprite Library

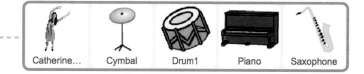

Catherine...   Cymbal   Drum1   Piano   Saxophone

STEP 3: Arrange all the sprites on the backdrop as shown. Click and drag the sprites to move them around your screen. (You might need to shrink the instruments to make them all fit.)

STEP 4: Add the below code to the Scripts section of your person sprite to make him/her move. Then open the sprite's information box (by clicking on the small ⓘ) and change the rotation style to right-to-left so the sprite doesn't flip upside down when moving.

This sprite comes with dancing costumes, which makes coding the animation easy. All your sprite needs to do is wait a small amount of time—so it doesn't move too quickly—move a bit, and change costumes!

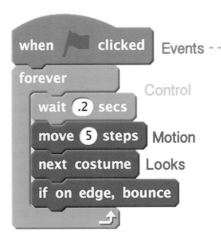

Events - - - - - This code starts when the green flag is clicked. The sprite will forever move, switch costumes (making it look like it's dancing), and wait a moment before repeating again. The *if on edge bounce* block prevents the sprite from moving off the screen when it gets to the edge.

STEP 5: Select a button sprite from the Sprite Library. In the Costumes tab, use the text tool to add the words *play all* to the button. Then add the below code to the button sprite's Scripts tab.

when this sprite clicked `Events` - - - - - You will need to create a new
broadcast Play ▼   message for the play broadcast.

STEP 6: Add the below code to the piano sprite. If you play piano, are musical, or just want to get creative, feel free to change the notes to a combination that you like. Otherwise just copy the notes you see here!

when this sprite clicked `Events` - - - This code is activated when the piano sprite is clicked.
set tempo to (60) bpm `Sound`   But you also want the piano to play when the *play all*
repeat (10) `Control`   button is pressed and the *play* broadcast is received.
  play note (60▼) for (0.5) beats
  play note (64▼) for (0.5) beats   Use the stamp tool to duplicate - - - - - - - when I receive Play ▼ `Events`
  play note (67▼) for (0.5) beats   the entire code block. Then (on the   set tempo to (60) bpm `Sound`
play note (67▼) for (0.5) beats   duplicate) pull off everything below   repeat (10) `Control`
play note (64▼) for (0.5) beats   the start command. Discard the   play note (60▼) for (0.5) beats
play note (60▼) for (0.5) beats   original start command and add   play note (64▼) for (0.5) beats
                                             a *when I receive play* block to the   play note (67▼) for (0.5) beats
                                             top. The code under both start   play note (67▼) for (0.5) beats
                                             commands will be identical.   play note (64▼) for (0.5) beats
                                                                                      play note (60▼) for (0.5) beats

play note (60▼) for (0.5) beats   The numbers in the *play note* block

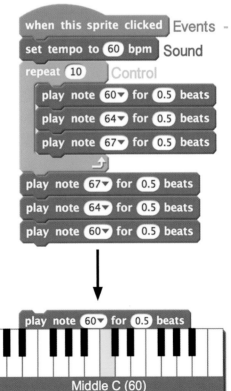

Middle C (60)

represent the note's pitch. Pitch is how high or low a note is. The higher the number, the higher the pitch! To select the proper note, click on the drop-down arrow to open the keyboard.

STEP 7: Add both code blocks from step 6 to the saxophone sprite. (The first one will be identical to the code on the piano except for the first **Sound** block.) Don't forget to change instrument to *saxophone* in that block.

Click the arrow to open the drop-down menu and select the instrument.

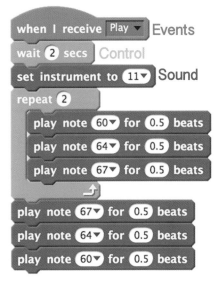

The second set of code will also need a *wait* command before the sounds play. (This will tell the instruments to start in rounds when they play together.) Add a wait command (2 seconds) below the *when I receive play* start command. Then change the *set tempo to* block to *set instrument to.* Don't forget to change the instrument to saxophone!

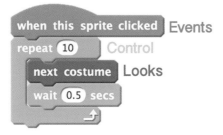

Add these two new blocks to the saxophone's Scripts tab. (The blocks are identical, except for their start commands, so it's easy to create one, duplicate it with the stamp tool, and swap out the first block.) These tell the sprite to switch costumes when clicked or when the play broadcast is received.

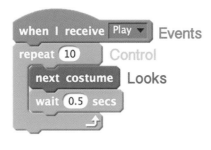

There will be a total of four code blocks on the saxophone when you are finished with step 7—two with the *play* broadcast start command and two with the *sprite clicked* start command. Running two sets of code under the same start command is called **parallel processing**. This is used when you need two things to start and run at the same time.

TIP:
You can copy the code blocks from the piano sprite to your saxophone sprite to save time. Just use your mouse pointer to select the entire code block you want to copy and drag it to hover over your saxophone sprite. When you let go, the code will bounce back to the Scripts section and be loaded to the saxophone.

STEP 8: Add this code to the cymbal sprite. Since the cymbal automatically comes with another costume, you will use parallel processing again to make the sprite play sounds and switch costumes when it's clicked.

Use the stamp tool to duplicate the top two code blocks. Then swap out the *when this sprite clicked* start commands for the *when I receive* start commands from Events. You should have four code blocks on the cymbal at the end of step 8.

The cymbal sounds are already in the Sounds tab for this sprite, so you don't need to add them.

STEP 9: Add this code to one of the *drum* sprites. Then use the stamp tool to duplicate the code. On the duplicate, swap out the start command for the *when I receive play* start command and add a one-second wait block from Control.

These blocks tell the drum sprite to play the selected notes—choose what you'd like or use what's shown here. Some notes will repeat if you add a loop. Get creative and make a beat all your own using the *play note* blocks from **Sound**.

STEP 10: Add this code to the second drum sprite.

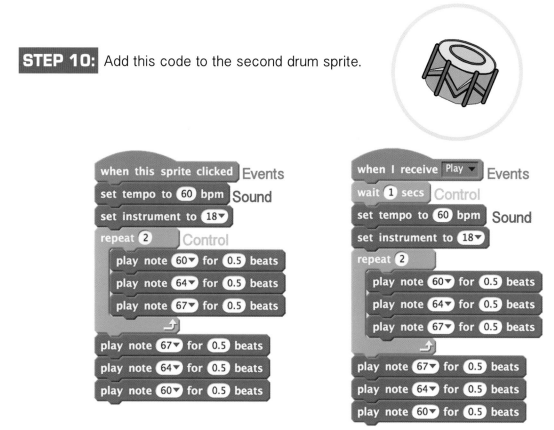

View your project in full-screen mode to see your band in action! Click the green flag, then press on the individual instruments to hear them play, or press the *play all* button to hear them all play together and watch your person dance! See the finished project here: https://scratch.mit.edu/projects/174112647/

Scared Ghost

THE PROJECT:

Watch as the ghost flies through a starry sky. See what happens when you make a loud sound and scare the ghost!

LET'S GET STARTED!

STEP 1: Start a new project and delete Scratch Cat. (Make sure to name and save your project!) In your backdrop screen, create a dark night sky and a small amount of grass/ground at the bottom.

scissors

paintbrush

 Use the paint bucket tool to fill in the sky black.

 Use the filled-in green rectangle to make a small patch of ground on the bottom of the backdrop. Don't worry about drawing stars—those will be added later as sprites.

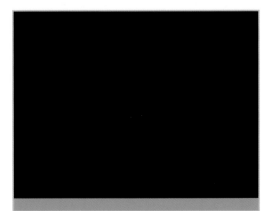

STEP 2: Open the Sprite Library and select *Ghost1.*

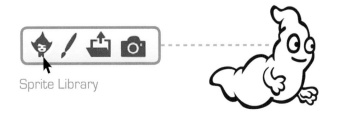

Sprite Library

STEP 3: Use the paintbrush icon in the new sprite toolbar to create a new sprite. (Before you go any further, click *convert to vector* at the bottom of the screen—this will let you reshape the shapes you need to draw.) Then follow these steps to draw a pumpkin sprite:

paintbrush

 Use the circle tool to draw a filled-in orange circle.

Click the reshape icon, then click on the orange circle to make the reshape dots appear. Move the sizing dots around to create a pumpkin-like shape. Pull the top dot down a bit. Then pull the bottom dots out to create a flatter bottom.

 Use the pencil tool and the color brown to draw lines on the pumpkin. Then use the square tool to draw a little stem on the top of the pumpkin.

When you're finished, open the sprite's information and name it *pumpkin*. Then change the rotation style to the right-to-left rotation.

STEP 4: Use the paintbrush icon to create a new sprite. Then use the paintbrush tool to draw a cluster of five to eight stars. (You might need to change the thickness of the paintbrush at the bottom of the screen.) Make sure you draw the stars close to the little cross in the drawing section; don't spread them out too much!

Name this sprite *stars*. Select the right-to-left rotation style in its information section.

stars

x: 185 y: 134   direction: -90°

rotation style: ↻ ↔ ●

can drag in player: ▢

show: ☑

STEP 5: Add the below code to the Scripts sections of both the *pumpkin* and *stars* sprites. This will make it look like the stars and the pumpkin are scrolling across the screen.

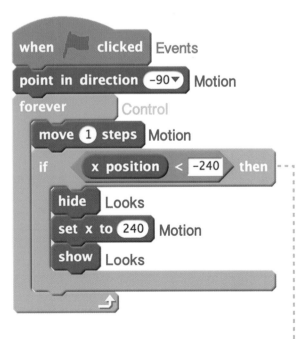

When the green flag is clicked, the sprites face the left of the screen. Then they will forever move one step, and if their *X* positions become less than -240 (the farthest spot on the left of the screen), the sprites will hide, set *X* to 240 (the farthest spot on the right of the screen), and show back up. They will continue moving, getting to the end of the screen, hiding, repositioning, and showing as long as the project is playing!

Use a *less than* block from Operators and a **Motion** block to build this piece of code. Then drop it inside your larger Control block.

STEP 6: Use the stamp tool at the top of the screen to duplicate the *stars* and *pumpkin* sprites until you have three stars sprites and four pumpkin sprites. (These duplicates will already have all the code you added in step 5.) When you're finished, arrange the sprites on the screen as shown. (Use the shrink or grow tools to adjust the size of the pumpkins so they're not all identical.)

TIP:
You can build this code block on one sprite and copy it to the other sprite to save time. (See page 27 if you need a reminder on how to do this.)

Imagine your Scratch work space is a big coordinate plane.

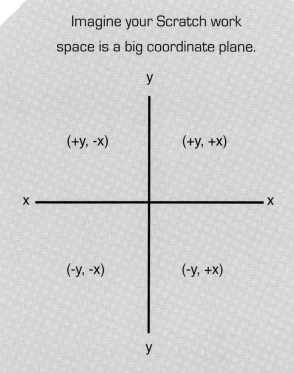

Changing the *X* and *Y* in the **Motion** block refers to the *X* and *Y* axis of a coordinate plane. If you have a positive *Y* coordinate, it will be found on the upper half of the plane. If you have a negative *Y* coordinate, it will be found on the lower half. If you have a positive *X* coordinate, it will be found on the right side. If you have a negative *X* coordinate, it will be found on the left side.

A **quadrant** is any of the four quarters into which something is divided by two real or imaginary lines (in this case, the X and Y axes) that intersect each other at right angles.

As you move your mouse around the plane, the *X* and *Y* coordinates on the bottom will change to show the mouse coordinates. X:0 Y:0 indicates that you are in the middle of the screen or coordinate plane. This is the **origin**.

STEP 7: Add the below code to the Scripts section of your ghost sprite. Since the sprites around the ghost will be moving, this will create the illusion that the ghost is flying through the air. In reality, the ghost will just bounce up and down in place!

```
when [flag] clicked    Events
forever    Control
    glide 1 secs to x: 0 y: 0
    glide 1 secs to x: 0 y: 10    Motion
```

When the green flag is clicked, the ghost sprite will forever glide from the center of the screen (x:0 y:0) to a spot slightly above it (x:0 y:10). This makes the ghost look like it's flying!

When the green flag is clicked, if the loudness is greater than 10, then the ghost will forever hide for two seconds, then show and say, *You scared me!* (You can adjust the loudness number to be more or less sensitive if needed.)

```
when [flag] clicked    Events
forever    Control
    if < loudness > 10 > then
        hide    Looks
        wait 2 secs    Control
        show    Looks
        say You scared me! for 2 secs
```

Use a *greater than* block from Operators and the *loudness* block from **Sensing** to build this piece of code. Then drop it inside your larger Control block. When you pull the *loudness* block out of **Sensing**, you will be asked to allow access to the microphone. Make sure you press *allow.* This will let you interact with the ghost using sounds you make!

Extras: To make the stars change color as they scroll across the screen, add the *change color effect by __* block to your stars sprite(s). To make the colors change faster, increase the number.

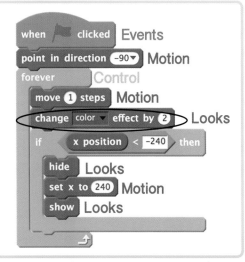

```
when [flag] clicked    Events
point in direction -90    Motion
forever    Control
    move 1 steps    Motion
    change color effect by 2    Looks
    if < x position < -240 > then
        hide    Looks
        set x to 240    Motion
        show    Looks
```

View your project in full-screen mode and click the green flag to start. Watch as the ghost flies through the sky—see what happens if you make a loud noise. See the finished project here: https://scratch.mit.edu/projects/174317731/

Tempo Bounce

THE PROJECT:

Set the tempo of the ball to see how quickly it moves. What happens to the ball if you increase the tempo?

LET'S GET STARTED!

STEP 1: Start a new project, and delete Scratch Cat. Create a new backdrop, and use the paint bucket tool to fill in the background with a solid color. Use the square tool (not filled in) to create an outline around the edges of your backdrop in a different solid color.

scissors   paintbrush

STEP 2: Open the Sprite Library and select the ball sprite. Then go to the sprite's Costumes tab and use the paint bucket to change the color of the ball. (Or select a ball from the different costumes already attached to the sprite.)

Sprite Library

STEP 3: Open the Sprite Library again and select the button sprite. In the Costumes tab, use the paint bucket to change the button's color and use the text tool to add the words *Change Tempo*.

CHANGE TEMPO

STEP 4: Go to the button sprite's Scripts tab and navigate to the Data category. Click *make a variable* and name it *tempo*. (We'll need this variable later in the project.)

CHANGE TEMPO

Make a Variable

New Variable

Variable name: tempo

● For all sprites   ○ For this sprite only

OK   Cancel

STEP 5: Add the below code to the button sprite. Then open the sprite's information section and name it *tempo*.

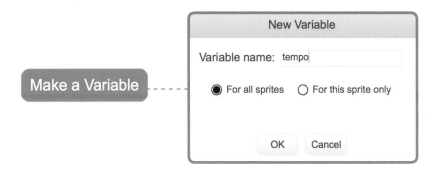

when this sprite clicked — Events

ask What would you like the tempo to be? and wait — Sensing

set Tempo to answer — Data / Sensing

The *ask and wait* code block lets you incorporate user input into your project. When this button is pressed, a bar will pop up that lets the user type in what they want the tempo to be. The *tempo* variable will then be set to that answer.

WHAT IS TEMPO?

Tempo refers to the speed of music being played. It is sometimes referred to as the beat! Listen to the beat the ball makes as it touches the edges and plays the pop sound. That's the ball's tempo.

STEP 6: Add the below code blocks to the ball sprite.

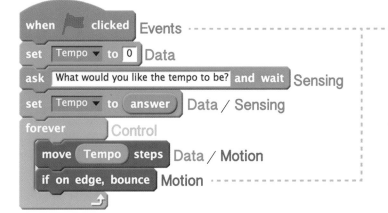

This code tells the ball sprite to move from side to side on the screen at a certain speed. When the green flag is clicked, the tempo is set to zero, and the user is asked to set the tempo. Once the tempo is set, the ball will forever move that number of steps and bounce off the edges.

The code tells the ball sprite to play the *pop* sound when it touches the outline on the screen. The code is activated when the green flag is clicked. Forever, if the ball touches the color blue and the tempo is less than 10, the *pop* sound will play and there will be a one-second wait. (This is so the sound doesn't play twice when the ball is going over the color blue.)

There is no wait block on the bottom section of code because when the tempo is higher, the ball will move faster. You don't have to worry about the *pop* sound playing twice.

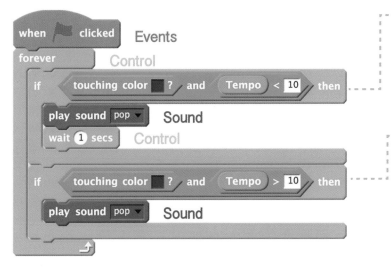

Build these larger blocks by first pulling the necessary blocks from Operators, **Sensing**, and **Data**. Combine them separately, then drop that block into the Control block.

To select the color for the **Sensing** block, click inside the *touching color* square. A small white finger cursor will appear. Move the cursor to the color you'd like to select—in this case the border around your screen—and click on it.

View your project in full-screen mode to see your game in action. Click the flag to start, then set and change the tempo of the ball to see how quickly it moves. See the finished project here: https://scratch.mit.edu/projects/174318688/

Soundboard

THE PROJECT:

Click the different buttons to hear the sounds or pictures they represent! Record your own sounds, use sounds from Scratch, or upload new sounds to create the best soundboard ever!

LET'S GET STARTED!

STEP 1: Create and name a new project. Use the scissors to delete Scratch Cat, then use the paintbrush icon in your backdrop toolbar to create a new backdrop.

scissors

paintbrush

 Use the paint bucket to fill in the background with a solid color.

STEP 2: Use the paintbrush icon in your sprite toolbar to create a sprite that will describe how to use the soundboard. Use the text tool to add the words for the sprite. (Make sure your text is a different color from your background so it's visible!)

Click the buttons to hear the sounds and see the characters that go with them!

Sprite Library

TIP:
Sprites don't always have to be characters—sometimes they can be words, like what you see here!

STEP 3: Select eight button sprites from the Sprite Library. (You can also select one and use the stamp tool to duplicate it until you have the correct amount.) Name each sprite (in its Costume tab) using a sound you want in your soundboard. Then use the text tool to add the same word onto the sprite.

stamp

STEP 4: Select a sprite to go with each button. You can select the sprite from the Sprite Library, edit a sprite in the library, or create your own! You should have a total of 17 sprites at the end of this step: eight button sprites, eight characters to go with the buttons, and one text sprite. We chose:

 Select *ghost2* from the Sprite Library.

 Select *ballerina* from the Sprite Library. (This sprite comes with multiple costumes, so you can easily animate her to dance!)

 Use the paintbrush icon (in bitmap mode) to create this sprite. Name it *crash*.

 Use the paintbrush icon (in vector mode) to create this sprite. Name it *gasp*.

 Select *heart face* from the Sprite Library.

 Select *Hannah* from the Sprite Library.

 Select *Pico walking* from the Sprite Library.

 Select *elephant* from the Sprite Library. In the Costumes tab, use the paintbrush to add tears and a puddle to make it look like he's crying.

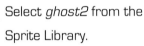

STEP 5: Arrange the button sprites to the backdrop as shown. Place the text sprite from step 2 next to the buttons. Then stack all the character sprites, one on top of the other, in the open space next to the buttons.

You will code the sprites to disappear and reappear at the correct time so they won't look cluttered when you are finished.

 Use the grow/shrink tools to adjust the sizes of the sprites to your liking.

STEP 6: Open the Sound Library for each button sprite (except for *kiss* and *gasp*) and choose sounds to go with the buttons.

New sound:

Sound Library

Sound Library

Category
All
Animal
Effects
Electronic
Human
Instruments
Music Loops
Musical Notes
Percussion
Vocals

Select the *Human* category to help find the sounds in the Sound Library. All the sounds needed for this step—except for kick drum, which is in the percussion category—can be found there.

Add the below code blocks to the *scream*, *crash*, *clapping*, *kick*, and *laugh* buttons. These codes will broadcast a message and make a sound when the sprite is pressed.

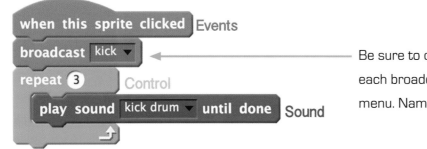

Be sure to create a new message for each broadcast using the drop-down menu. Name them to match the button.

STEP 7: There are no sounds in the Sound Library for *kiss* and *gasp* so you'll need to record those before adding the below code.

microphone

Click on the microphone in the Sounds tab of either sprite and record the correct sound. (Refer to page 15 for a refresher on how to record a sound if you need help.)

After you've finished recording, you might need to use the edit tools. You can shorten your sound if it's too long, or make it louder if it's too quiet. When you're happy with your sound, change the name from *recording1* to either *kiss* or *gasp*. Repeat for other sounds.

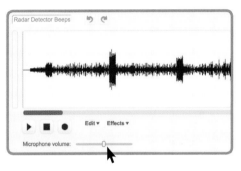

This code will activate when the buttons are clicked, broadcast a message, and then play a sound!

STEP 8: Next add the sound to the crying button sprite. You'll be uploading a sound from your computer.

The crying sound for this project should only be a few seconds long. If the sound is too long, highlight the section of the sound that you need to remove and trim it. (For a refresher on how to do this, go page 17.) When you are done editing the sound, rename it *crying*.

TIP:
Don't forget to credit the sound's creator in your project. Below the download buttons is a list of information, including who recorded each sound. That's where you'll find who to credit.

STEP 9: Add this code to the crying button sprite:

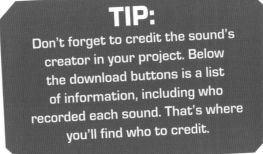

STEP 10: Add this code to the text sprite:

Click the buttons to hear the sounds and see the characters that go with them!

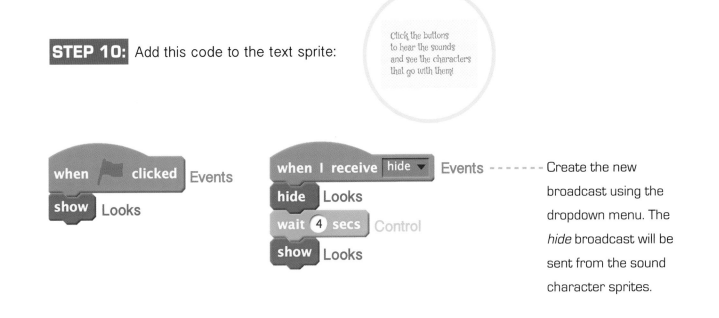

when [flag] clicked Events
show Looks

when I receive [hide ▼] Events - - - - - - - Create the new
hide Looks
wait (4) secs Control
show Looks

broadcast using the dropdown menu. The *hide* broadcast will be sent from the sound character sprites.

STEP 11: Code each of the character sprites you see here with the below code blocks:

when [flag] clicked Events
hide Looks

when I receive [cry ▼] Events
broadcast [hide ▼] Events
show Looks
wait (3) secs Control
hide Looks

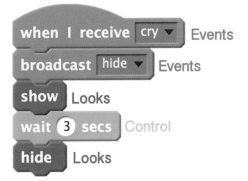

This code will be the same on all the character sprites (except for *Pico* and *ballerina*). The only change in the code from sprite to sprite will be the start command. Make sure the start command matches with the character you're coding. (Example: The elephant sprite will start when it receives *cry.*)

Since *Pico* and *ballerina* have different costumes, which make them easy to animate, their code blocks will be slightly different. When they receive the appropriate broadcast, they will show, change costumes, and then hide. The repeat block tells the costumes to change a certain number of times (however many you put inside the repeat loop), and the wait block makes sure the costumes don't change too quickly.

Make sure the start command for Pico is changed to *when I receive laugh*, and the switch costume says *Pico walk 1*!

TIP:

To copy code from one sprite to another, grab the code from the top block and move it to the center of the sprite you're trying to code. Then let go. The code will be copied onto the sprite you held the code over.

View your project in full-screen mode and click the green flag to start. Click on the different buttons to hear the matching sounds and see the matching characters! See the finished project here: https://scratch.mit.edu/projects/174315736/

Read More

Wainewright, Max. *Code Your Own Games!: 20 Games to Create with Scratch*. New York, NY. Sterling Children's Books, 2017.

Ziter, Rachel. *Animation and Presentation from Scratch: 4D An Augmented Reading Experience*. North Mankato, Minn.: Capstone Press, 2019.

Ziter, Rachel. *Coding in Scratch for Beginners: 4D An Augmented Reading Experience*. North Mankato, Minn.: Capstone Press, 2018.

Makerspace Tips

Download tips and tricks for using this book and others in a library makerspace.

Visit www.capstonepub.com/dabblelabresources

Internet Sites

Use Facthound to find Internet sites related to this book.

Visit www.facthound.com

Just type in 9781515766605 and go.

Coding Glossary

bitmap mode: The drawing tools in this mode make it easy to fill in backgrounds and shapes. If you are making a quick shape or basic background, bitmap mode is a good choice. (Keep in mind that if you need to go back and resize a shape later, bitmap mode won't allow it.) To change between bitmap and vector mode, use the buttons on the bottom right of the design screen.

broadcast: These code blocks can be found in the Events category of the Scripts tab. A broadcast is like sending a message.

coding: Coding is the language used to communicate with a computer. By creating a set of code, you are writing directions in a language that the computer can follow. Code is very specific! Without code, computers wouldn't know how to do anything.

conditional statement: A conditional statement is used in code when you need one thing to happen, but only if another does. (For example: If _____ happens, then _____ needs to happen.) These are also called *if then* statements.

coordinate: A coordinate is an object's exact X-position and Y-position on a coordinate plane. Think of it as a very specific spot!

coordinate plane: A coordinate plane is made up of an X and Y axis. These two axes run perpendicular to each other—one runs up and down, and the other runs right to left. When they meet, the axes create four quadrants.

loop: Loops are used in coding when something needs to happen more than once. Loops can be used with one piece of code or many. The code inside the loop will run (on repeat) in the order it's placed in.

origin: The origin is the middle point of a coordinate plane. This is where the X-coordinate and Y-coordinate both equal zero and the two axes cross.

sequence: Sequence is when something is completed in a specific order. In coding, all programs run in a sequence from top to bottom, meaning the top piece of code will be run first, then the block under it, until the sequence is complete.

sprite: A sprite is any moveable character or object used in a Scratch project. Sprites can be selected through the Scratch Library, created using drawing tools, or uploaded from the computer.

variable: A variable is a placeholder for a value and can be made in the Data category of the Scripts tab. The value of a variable can be changed throughout the course of a project. For example, if a variable was used for the number of lives in a game, you could set it to three at the start of a game. Then each time one sprite touches a certain sprite, the lives variable can be coded to decrease by one.

vector mode: The drawing tools in this mode are similar to tools in bitmap mode. However, in vector mode you can create another shape and still go back to a previous one and move it. In this mode, you can also reshape objects that you have made.

X-axis: The X-axis is the axis that runs horizontally (side to side) in a coordinate plane.

Y-axis: The Y-axis is the axis that runs vertically (up and down) in a coordinate plane.

ABOUT THE AUTHOR

Rachel Ziter was raised in Las Vegas, Nevada. She earned a Bachelor of Science in Education and her teaching credentials from Florida Southern College. She has also completed graduate coursework in computer science education at St. Scholastica, as well as professional development in fablab project-based learning at NuVu. Rachel currently works at the Adelson Educational Campus in Las Vegas and is a member of the Tech Team, where she teaches STEM curriculum and instruction, mentors students, and teaches coding and engineering.